SPACE FACTS AND FIGURES

EXPLORING SPACE

Nancy Dickmann

WINDMILL
BOOKS ™

Published in 2019 by **Windmill Books**, an imprint of Rosen Publishing
29 East 21ˢᵗ Street, New York, NY 10010

For Brown Bear Books Ltd:
Text and Editor: Nancy Dickmann
Children's Publisher: Anne O'Daly
Editorial Director: Lindsey Lowe
Design Manager: Keith Davis
Designer and Illustrator: Supriya Sahai
Picture Manager: Sophie Mortimer

Concept development: Square and Circus/Brown Bear Books Ltd

Picture Credits:
Front cover: Supriya Sahai
Dreamstime: Photographerlondon 5; iStock: Sylphe_7 26; NASA: Ames/JPL-Caltech 24cr, ARC 18,
ESA/JPL/Srizona State Univ 25, JHUAPL/SwRI 20, 21, 28t, 29b, JPL 12, 13, 23, JPL-Caltech 15, 17, 29t,
JPL 22, JPL/ESA 16, JSC 4, TRW 24cl; Shutterstock: 3Dsculptor 9, 28b, Castieski 7, Marcel Clemens
10, Elenarts 18-19, Everett Historical 6, Vadim Sadovski 24l; Wikipedia: Jeff Foust 27, NASA 11, 14,
NASA/JPL-Caltech 24r.

Key: t=top, b=bottom, c=center, l=left, r=right

Brown Bear Books has made every attempt to contact the copyright holder.
If anyone has any information please contact licensing@brownbearbooks.co.uk

Cataloging-in-Publication Data

Names: Dickmann, Nancy.
Title: Exploring space / Nancy Dickmann.
Description: New York : Windmill Books, 2019. | Series: Space facts and figures |
Includes glossary and index.
Identifiers: LCCN ISBN 9781508195115 (pbk.) | ISBN 9781508195108 (library bound) |
ISBN 9781508195122 (6 pack)
Subjects: LCSH: Manned space flight--Juvenile literature. |
Outer space--Exploration--Juvenile literature.
Classification: LCC QB500.262 D53 2019 | DDC 629.45--dc23

Manufactured in the United States of America

CPSIA Compliance Information: Batch #BS18WM:
For Further Information contact Rosen Publishing, New York, New York at 1-800-237-9932

CONTENTS

WHAT'S OUT THERE?

Space is huge and full of mysteries. Scientists use telescopes and spacecraft to find out more about it.

So far, **astronauts** have not traveled farther than the **moon**. **Astronomers** can study objects that are farther away by using **telescopes**. We also send robotic spacecraft to explore. Robotic spacecraft have visited all the **planets** in the **solar system**. Some have landed on distant worlds.

Robotic spacecraft have traveled to the edge of the solar system.

Our solar system is a tiny part of an enormous **galaxy**.

Today's astronauts only travel about 250 miles (400 kilometers) from Earth.

Powerful telescopes on Earth can study distant galaxies.

Even just binoculars or a simple telescope will give you a good view of space.

GO FIGURE!

Date of first human spaceflight:
April 12, 1961
Length of first human spaceflight:
1 hour 48 minutes
Planets in the solar system (other than Earth): 7
Number visited by astronauts so far: 0

VISITING THE MOON

The moon is the only object in space that humans have visited. Six missions landed there in the 1960s and 70s.

On July 20, 1969, Neil Armstrong became the first person to step onto the moon. Over the next three and a half years, 11 other astronauts followed. They performed experiments and studied the moon's surface. They brought samples of moon rock back to earth.

The moon missions were launched on enormous Saturn V rockets.

Three of the moon missions used a motorized buggy.

The missions that sent astronauts to the moon were the Apollo program.

Each Apollo mission had a crew of three astronauts.

Lunar module

When the spacecraft returned to Earth, they landed in the ocean.

GO FIGURE!

Distance from Earth to moon: 238,855 miles (384,400 kilometers)
Average journey time: about 3 days
Total moon rocks brought back by Apollo astronauts: 842 pounds (382 kilograms)
Last astronaut on the moon: December 14, 1972

SPACE SHUTTLE

The space shuttle was a reusable spacecraft. It took people, satellites, and other equipment into space.

The shuttle took off like a rocket. It flew back and landed like an airplane. Giant rockets sent it into space. Engines on the shuttle helped to steer it. Astronauts stayed on the shuttle for about 10 days. They did experiments on board. The first shuttle was launched in 1985. In total the shuttles made 135 trips into space.

Five shuttles went into space. They were Atlantis, Challenger, Columbia, Discovery, and Endeavour.

The shuttle traveled at up to 17,400 miles (28,000 kilometers) per hour!

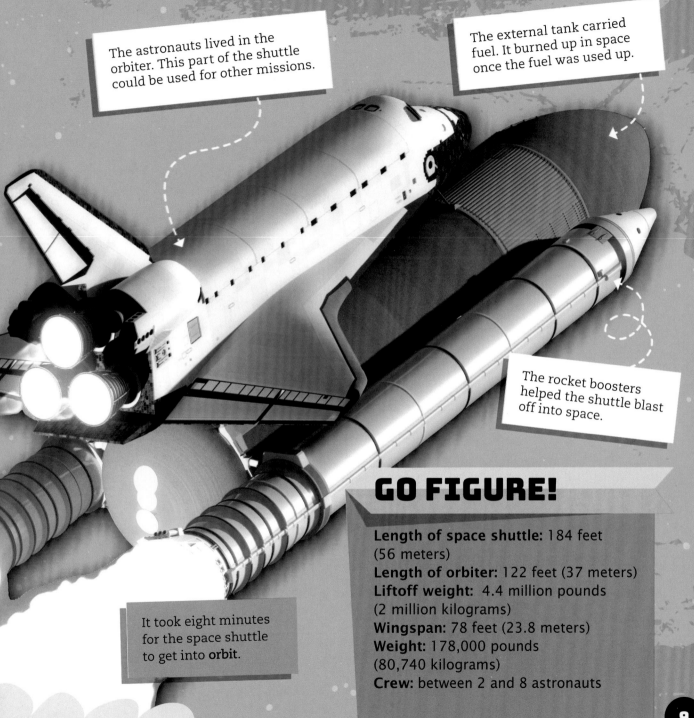

The astronauts lived in the orbiter. This part of the shuttle could be used for other missions.

The external tank carried fuel. It burned up in space once the fuel was used up.

The rocket boosters helped the shuttle blast off into space.

It took eight minutes for the space shuttle to get into **orbit**.

GO FIGURE!

Length of space shuttle: 184 feet (56 meters)
Length of orbiter: 122 feet (37 meters)
Liftoff weight: 4.4 million pounds (2 million kilograms)
Wingspan: 78 feet (23.8 meters)
Weight: 178,000 pounds (80,740 kilograms)
Crew: between 2 and 8 astronauts

INTERNATIONAL SPACE STATION

The space shuttle is good for short visits. If you want to stay longer in space, you need a space station.

Engineers from several countries helped to build the International Space Station (ISS). The first section was launched in 1998. More sections were added over the years. Astronauts from around the world live and work on the space station. They perform scientific experiments and learn more about living without **gravity**.

The ISS can be seen from Earth without a telescope.

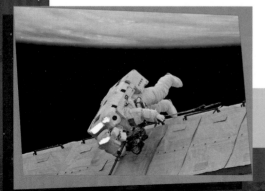

An astronaut on a spacewalk outside the ISS.

Spacecraft take astronauts and cargo to and from the space station.

Overall length: 357 feet (109 meters)
Overall mass: 925,335 pounds (419,725 kilograms)
Solar panel wingspan: 240 feet (73 meters)
Electrical wiring: 8 miles (13 kilometers) in total

Eight **solar panel** arrays capture the sun's energy to provide electricity.

Solar panel array

The solar arrays can fold up like accordions for transportation.

The space station has a robotic arm that can lift a space shuttle.

11

MERCURY AND VENUS

There are two planets between Earth and the sun: Mercury and Venus. They have been studied by robotic spacecraft.

Mercury and Venus are both too hot for astronauts to visit. The robotic MESSENGER spacecraft mapped Mercury's surface and learned more about the inside of the planet. Many spacecraft have visited Venus. A few even landed on the surface, but they were destroyed by high **temperature** and **pressure**.

The *Magellan* spacecraft used **radar** to "see" through thick clouds on Venus.

MESSENGER

MESSENGER had a heat shield for protection against Mercury's high temperatures.

Only two spacecraft, Mariner 10 and MESSENGER, have ever visited Mercury.

GO FIGURE!

MESSENGER's heat shield:
8 feet (2.5 meters) tall and 6 feet
(2 meters) wide
MESSENGER's mass: 1,120 pounds
(508 kilometers)
Mercury closest distance to Earth:
48 million miles (77 million kilometers)
Venus closest distance to Earth:
24 million miles (38 million kilometers)

Mercury

Several spacecraft have flown past Venus on their way to the outer solar system.

MARS ROVERS

Mars has been visited by many spacecraft. Some of them have driven around on the surface!

Most rovers have solar panels to keep their batteries charged.

The first Mars **rover** was *Sojourner*. It landed in 1997. It explored the planet for about three months. The twin rovers *Spirit* and *Opportunity* arrived in 2004. The biggest and most complex rover is *Curiosity*. It landed on Mars in 2012. Rovers can drill into rocks to learn more about the planet.

Solar panel

NASA scientists running tests on a Mars rover before launch

The rovers search for evidence of water and life on Mars.

GO FIGURE!

Sojourner mass: 23 pounds (10.6 kilograms)
Spirit/Opportunity mass: 384 pounds (174 kilograms)
Curiosity mass: 1,982 pounds (899 kilograms)
Curiosity distance driven: 10.66 miles (17.16 kilometers) as of August 2017

Camera

Antenna

Curiosity is the size of a large car.

Six tough wheels let Curiosity roll over objects up to 25 inches (65 centimeters) high.

Curiosity's robotic arm can reach objects 7 feet (2 meters) away.

CASSINI

Saturn sits at the center of a system of rings and moons. The spacecraft Cassini has explored it all in detail.

Cassini entered orbit around Saturn in 2004. It studied the planet's clouds. It dived through its rings and studied its moons. It found icy fountains spewing out of the moon Enceladus. *Cassini* released a **lander** called *Huygens*, which landed on the surface of Saturn's moon Titan. *Cassini* crashed into Saturn in September 2017, sending back pictures and data until the very end.

Cassini showed that rain on Titan is made of liquid methane.

This is an artist's picture of the place where *Huygens* landed on Titan.

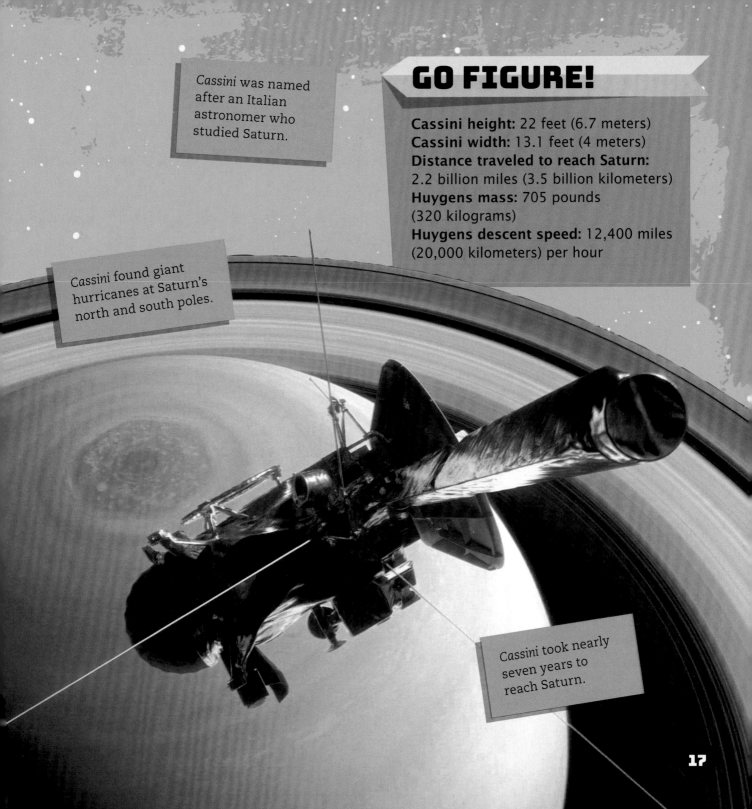

Cassini was named after an Italian astronomer who studied Saturn.

GO FIGURE!

Cassini height: 22 feet (6.7 meters)
Cassini width: 13.1 feet (4 meters)
Distance traveled to reach Saturn: 2.2 billion miles (3.5 billion kilometers)
Huygens mass: 705 pounds (320 kilograms)
Huygens descent speed: 12,400 miles (20,000 kilometers) per hour

Cassini found giant hurricanes at Saturn's north and south poles.

Cassini took nearly seven years to reach Saturn.

VOYAGER

More than 40 years ago, twin spacecraft were launched. They are now exploring the very edges of the solar system.

Voyager 1 and Voyager 2 both launched in 1977. Voyager 1 flew past Jupiter and Saturn before heading to the outer solar system. Voyager 2 followed a slightly different path. After passing Jupiter and Saturn, it sent back the first detailed photos of Uranus and Neptune. Both spacecraft are still sending back data as they travel into deep space.

Voyager 2 is the only spacecraft to study all four of the outer planets.

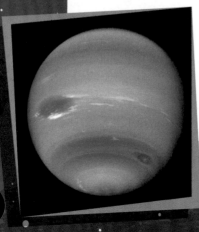

Voyager 2 took this picture of Neptune.

Antenna

Both spacecraft carry photos and sound recordings of life on Earth.

Voyager 2 discovered 10 moons and 2 rings around Uranus.

Voyager 1 also flew past Saturn's moon Titan.

GO FIGURE!

Voyager size: 5 feet 10 inches (1.78 meters) wide and 18.5 inches (47 centimeters) high
Antenna size: 12 feet (3.66 meters) wide
Voyager 2 distance traveled: nearly 11 billion miles (17.7 billion kilometers)
Voyager 1 speed: 38,027 miles (61,198 kilometers) per hour

Voyager 1 discovered a system of faint rings around Jupiter.

Jupiter

19

NEW HORIZONS

Pluto is small, cold, and very far away. In 2015, it was finally explored up close, thanks to the New Horizons spacecraft.

When *New Horizons* launched in 2006, Pluto was known as the ninth planet of the solar system. Later that year, astronomers decided that Pluto was a **dwarf planet** instead. *New Horizons* sent back photos and information about this icy world and its moons. Its next mission is to study other icy objects in the outer solar system.

New Horizons is about the size of a baby grand piano.

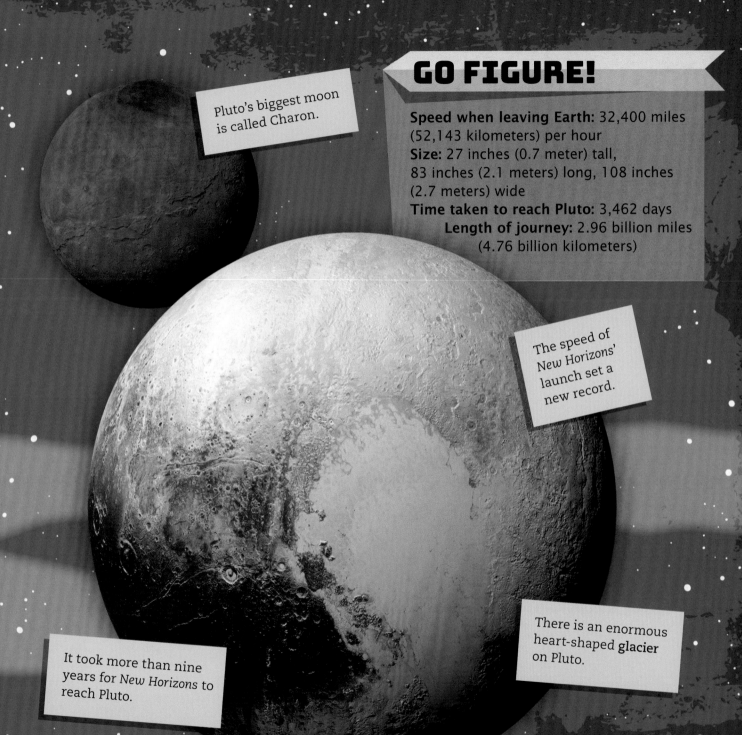

Pluto's biggest moon is called Charon.

GO FIGURE!

Speed when leaving Earth: 32,400 miles (52,143 kilometers) per hour
Size: 27 inches (0.7 meter) tall, 83 inches (2.1 meters) long, 108 inches (2.7 meters) wide
Time taken to reach Pluto: 3,462 days
Length of journey: 2.96 billion miles (4.76 billion kilometers)

The speed of *New Horizons'* launch set a new record.

It took more than nine years for *New Horizons* to reach Pluto.

There is an enormous heart-shaped **glacier** on Pluto.

COMET CATCHERS

Comets hurtle through the solar system at great speed. Landing on one is very tricky. But in 2014, a spacecraft did just that.

Rosetta was looking for **molecules** that form the building blocks of life.

Comets sometimes pass close to Earth. But to get a more detailed look we need to send spacecraft. The Stardust mission brought back dust samples from a comet's tail in 2003. The Rosetta mission topped that by going into orbit around Comet 67P. It sent down a lander called *Philae* to learn more about the comet.

Stardust used a super-light material called aerogel to catch comet dust.

Some types of aerogels are 99.9% air.

GO FIGURE!

Stardust sample capsule: 30 inches (76 centimeters) by 20 inches (51 centimeters)
Stardust distance from Earth during comet encounter: 242 million miles (389 million kilometers)
Grains of dust from outside the solar system: 7
Rosetta dimensions: 110 inches (2.8 meters) by 83 inches (2.1 meters) by 79 inches (2.0 meters)

Comet 67P

Philae bounced when it landed and ended up in a dark crack.

Rosetta orbited the comet for more than two years.

SPACE TELESCOPES

Telescopes on the ground can peer far into space. Space telescopes in orbit around Earth can see even better.

The first space telescope was Hubble. It was launched in 1990.

Earth is surrounded by a blanket of gases called the **atmosphere**. These gases partly block our view of space. Telescopes in orbit, above the atmosphere, have a clear view. As they circle Earth, they point out into the solar system. These space telescopes have studied galaxies and discovered planets orbiting other stars.

NASA's space telescopes

Hubble

Chandra

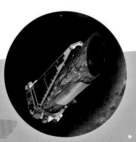
Kepler

Spitzer

It took astronauts about three days to travel to the moon.

One spacecraft crashed into the moon on purpose, to see what was in the dust that was thrown up.

Astronauts collected rock samples and did scientific experiments on the moon.

GO FIGURE!

First robotic landing on the moon: September 13, 1959 (Luna 2)
First human landing: July 20, 1969 (Apollo 11)
First robotic spacecraft to orbit moon: April 1966 (Luna 10)
First astronauts to orbit moon: December 1968 (Apollo 8)

Robotic spacecraft have found water ice on the moon.

25

OTHER MOONS

Earth is not the only planet that has a moon. Some planets have dozens of moons!

Mars has two small moons, but the outer planets have many more. Jupiter has the most moons of any planet. Other objects, such as asteroids and dwarf planets, can have moons too. All of the moons that astronomers have discovered so far are rocky or icy. Some have liquid oceans beneath the surface.

Ganymede is the biggest moon in our solar system.

Our moon, compared in size to some of Jupiter's moons

GANYMEDE   CALLISTO   IO   MOON   EUROPA

Jupiter's moon Ganymede and Saturn's moon Titan are both bigger than the planet Mercury.

Some moons are asteroids that were captured by a planet's gravity.

Jupiter

The spacecraft Huygens landed on Titan.

GO FIGURE!

Largest moon (Ganymede): 3,270 miles (5,262 kilometers) wide
Second-largest moon (Titan): 3,200 miles (5,150 kilometers) wide
Earth's moon size: 5th largest of all solar system moons
Moons of Jupiter: at least 69 discovered so far

Mercury and Venus are the only planets that do not have moons.

Astronomers are still finding new moons.

QUIZ

Try this quiz and test your knowledge of the moon!
The answers are on page 32.

1 What shape is the moon's orbit around Earth?

A. a perfect circle

B. a slightly squashed circle

C. a triangle

2 What is the moon's crust made of?

A. ice

B. cheese

C. rock

3 What happens when the moon passes directly between Earth and the sun?

A. it causes a solar eclipse

B. it appears as a full moon

C. it collects $200 from the banker

4 What holds the moon in orbit around Earth?

A. a really long rope

B. gravity

C. air pressure

5 What do we call the moon's shape when less than half of it is showing?

A. scrawny

B. croissant

C. crescent

6 What are the dark patches on the moon's surface?

A. low areas filled with solid lava

B. shadows cast by Earth

C. places where the cheese has gone moldy

7 Why are there so many craters on the moon?

A. it just hasn't found a good enough moisturizer

B. there is no atmosphere to protect the moon from space rocks

C. there is no one to sweep them away

8 What did astronauts do when they visited the moon?

A. hunted for aliens

B. collected rocks and did science experiments

C. sunbathed

GLOSSARY

asteroid a large chunk of rock left over from when the planets formed

astronaut person who travels into space

astronomer person who studies the sun, the planets, and other objects in space

atmosphere a layer of gas trapped by gravity around the surface of a planet, moon, or other object

core the center of a planet, moon, or some asteroids

crater circular hole made when a comet, asteroid, or meteorite hits a planet or moon

crust the hard outer layer of a rocky planet, moon, or some asteroids

dwarf planet object that is too small to be considered a planet, but too big to be an asteroid

eclipse when one object in space temporarily blocks out another

friction the action of one surface or object rubbing against another

gravity a force that pulls objects together. The heavier or closer an object is, the stronger its gravity, or pull.

lava melted rock that pours onto a planet's surface from underground

mantle the middle layer of some planets, moons, and asteroids

mare an area of low land on the moon that has been filled in with lava

mass the measure of the amount of material in an object

mineral a solid, natural, non-living substance

orbit the path an object takes around a larger object; or, to take such a path

phase one of the different shapes the moon appears as it travels around Earth

planet large, spherical object that orbits the sun or another star

solar system a group of planets that circles a star

telescope tool used for studying space, which gathers information about things that are far away

temperature measure of how hot or cold something is

tides the regular rising and falling of sea levels due to the moon's gravity

volcanoes mountains formed from lava that erupts onto the surface from underground

FURTHER RESOURCES

Books

Bredeson, Carmen. *Exploring the Moon (Launch Into Space!).* Enslow Publishers, 2015.

Gifford, Clive. *Astronomy, Astronauts, and Space Exploration (Watch This Space!).* Crabtree Publishing Company, 2015.

Simon, Seymour. *Our Solar System.* HarperCollins, 2014.

Taylor-Butler, Christine. *The Moon (New True Books: Space).* Scholastic, 2014.

Thimmesh, Catherine. *Team Moon: How 400,000 People Landed Apollo 11 on the Moon.* HMH Books for Young Readers, 2015.

Websites

For web resources related
to the subject of this book, go to:
www.windmillbooks.com/weblinks
and select this book's title.

INDEX

Answers to quiz:
1. b; 2. c; 3. a; 4. b; 5. c; 6. a; 7. b; 8. b